Client-Worker Transactions

LIBRARY OF SOCIAL WORK

GENERAL EDITOR: NOEL TIMMS
Professor of Applied Social Studies
University of Bradford

Client-Worker Transactions

by William Jordan

Lecturer and Tutor in Social Work
University of Exeter

LONDON
ROUTLEDGE & KEGAN PAUL

First published 1970
by Routledge & Kegan Paul Ltd
Broadway House, 68-74 Carter Lane
London E.C.4
Printed in Great Britain
by Northumberland Press Limited,
Gateshead
© William Jordan 1970

ISBN 0 7100 6836 0 (C)
ISBN 0 7100 6837 9 (P)

General editor's introduction

The Library of Social Work is designed to meet the needs of students following courses of training for social work. In recent years the number and kinds of training have increased in an unprecedented way. But there has been no corresponding increase in the supply of text-books to cover the growing differentiation of subject matter or to respond to the growing spirit of enthusiastic but critical enquiry into the range of subjects relevant to social work. The Library will consist of short texts designed to introduce the student to the main features of each topic of enquiry, to the significant theoretical contributions so far made to its understanding, and to some of the outstanding problems. Each volume will suggest ways in which the student might continue his work by further reading.

This book introduces a transactional approach to the relationship between social caseworker and client, and develops some criticisms of what William Jordan describes as the 'accepted theory' on these matters. The first chapter explores the significance of the fact that social work agencies provide both a public service for the community and offer help to individuals in trouble. To understand the relationships that social workers develop with their clients we have been accustomed to look to what happens in the psychoanalytic treatment situation, but, the author argues, this overlooks a crucial difference between the two. A social work agency provides a public service in respect of certain social problems and it does not characteristically invite its clientele to express their problems in the form of a conflict between internalized parental figures and infantile emotional needs. The author argues that it does invite what he terms 'defensive manoeuvres' by offering help with social problems. A defensive manoeuvre leads to a series of transactions with the worker which have as their objective getting the social worker to act out unwanted parts of the client's personality: '... the emotional transaction between client and worker is the expression of the social

v

problem within these roles which corresponds to the transference expression of the neurosis within the roles of patient and psychoanalyst.'

The idea of people getting others to act out unwanted 'parts' of themselves is not new in social work, but in the second chapter the author begins to show some of the difficulties inherent in the notion. He critically examines some of the writings of the (then) Family Discussion Bureau, particularly the possibility that one partner in a marriage gets the other to carry 'a double dose' of unwanted feeling. This, suggests William Jordan, implies some kind of unconscious communication, and he argues that this idea has been insufficiently explored. It is clearly a topic requiring much more work; particularly from the viewpoint of philosophical psychology, but the author has succeeded in identifying a problem of central concern to social workers, who are more concerned with what happens between people than with what takes place 'within' them.

In the third chapter the author turns to a second major criticism of the usual theory of the casework relationship, and considers the analogy frequently drawn between social work and medicine. Everything that the social worker does is seen as treatment, but what the client does is always a symptom. He suggests that casework theory is often unhelpful in guiding social work activity, particularly with disruptive clients. 'If casework theory fails to recognize that some people come to agencies with such covert aims as to seek rejection, to browbeat the worker, or imprison him, or scare him out of his wits, then it can provide the worker with little guidance as to how such people can be helped.'

This book is about casework 'treatment', though its transactional approach may well be useful to those more concerned with other social work methods. Obviously, casework treatment can be approached in a number of different ways, and more than one work devoted to that subject can be expected in the Library of Social Work (Jonathan Moffett has already analysed some of the concepts involved). This particular volume has links with the study of the application of Kleinian concepts to social work (Wittenberg), and it also makes a contribution to the study of social administration, since it is concerned with exploring the dynamic interaction of client, worker and agency. It begins also to indicate the basis and the method of at least one way in which social work theorizing might develop in the future. It uses fieldwork experience as a basis for the criticism of existing casework theory and as a means of developing it, and it relies heavily on case examples from the field which show the value of fieldwork experience recorded in a way that highlights for both clients and workers the meaning of their encounters.

NOEL TIMMS

Contents

1
Defensive manoeuvres and transactions

The professional relationship in social work

In this book I want to put forward a way of thinking about the relationship between a social worker and his client which is rather different from the one which has come to be generally accepted.

What I call the accepted way of thinking is based on a reconciliation of two different aspects of the social worker's task, the carrying out of an official function on behalf of the community, and the taking part in live relationships with individual people. This way of thinking recognizes the fact that social workers provide both a public service for the community in respect of certain social problems and an individual service to people with real needs and feelings, and it meets this difficulty with the notion of the professional relationship.

According to this notion, while the worker should always have in mind the function of his agency in his aims and methods of treatment, and while his relationship with the client should be directed towards helping him to solve the social problem which brings him to the agency, he should also recognize that the client will not respond rationally and unemotionally to his efforts to help him. 'If a person is in need and turns to another one for help, the helper takes on a symbolic role far beyond his actual significance as a real person.' (Goldberg, 1963.) The client 'tends to pin on to us attitudes that rightly belong to his childhood.' (Lloyd Davies, 1963.)

In descriptions of this emotional content of the relationship between worker and client the Freudian term 'transference' is often used. In psychoanalysis, feelings and phantasies which are aroused in the patient by the analyst are taken to be new editions of the same feelings and phantasies towards the patient's parents which he experienced during his childhood. It is usually assumed that the phenomenon seen in social work is the same as that which is encountered in the relationship between a psychoanalyst and his patient, even if it is not dealt with in the same way. 'Transference is of course the manifestation of unconscious phantasy, interfering with adaptation to reality.' It involves '... perceptual distortion, inappropriate emotion and manipulative action—its tendency to transform this present person and present situation into the image and likeness of an earlier person and a past situation.' (Irvine, 1963.)

However, there is an important difference between social work and psychoanalysis which affects the way in which this transference is regarded. In psychoanalysis the analyst's basic aim and method is quite simply to make conscious what is unconscious. The transference represents a very important manifestation of what is unconscious, and it is therefore a major task of treatment to make this conscious through interpretation. In social

2

work, however, there is no logical connection between the function of the agency (which may be to prevent family breakup, or to provide for the homeless) and the transference phenomenon. It is not part of the aim of a social work agency simply to make the unconscious conscious.

The accepted way of thinking deals with this by suggesting that the transference is only one side of the client's attitudes and feelings towards the worker. Besides this emotional side based on infantile emotional needs there is a rational, realistic side which recognizes the function of the agency and seeks its help. While the worker should be aware of the transference, he should seek to make use of these realistic elements in the relationship. 'We social caseworkers do not aim at radical personality changes but at changes in underlying attitudes which affect the individual's solving of his problems. This we attempt to do by mobilizing the healthy parts of the personality to try to set in motion the natural healing forces present in everyone.' (Lloyd Davies, 1963.) Hollis (1964) uses a similar metaphor, and writes of two different kinds of attitudes and responses by the client, the realistic and the unrealistic, the latter being the transference from parental relationships.

The difference between psychoanalytic theory and social work theory is important, because in psychoanalysis the transference is not just a resistance to treatment, it is also 'what is resisted', namely the unconscious. It is an expression of what it is that is being treated, and the making conscious of it constitutes a great deal of the treatment. But social work theory does not see the transference as an expression of what is to be treated, because the function of a social worker is to treat 'social problems'. A social problem, according to the accepted theory, arises when a person's emotional and psychological mechanisms fail to function in a way that enables him to adjust to the demands of the community in which he lives. When that person becomes aware that he is failing to adjust, he seeks help with his social problem, and the accepted theory sees this request for help as something which expresses those parts of his personality which are realistic, healthy and tending towards a better social adjustment. What then is the relationship between the social problem, the request for help and the transference?

According to the accepted theory, when a person becomes aware that he has a social problem, this gives rise both to the realistic desire for help from a social worker, and to the feelings of weakness, failure and dependence which go to make up the transference. These transference feelings are taken to arise from the parental position occupied by the social worker in this situation, and to co-exist alongside the realistic perception of him as someone who helps overcome the social problem.

It is at this point that the accepted theory seems to me to be confused. It assumes that the emotional content of the transference between client and social worker is similar in kind to that within the relationship between a patient and his psychoanalyst, namely an expression of unconscious infantile emotional needs and conflicts. But it ignores the fact that psychoanalysis, because it sees the patient's illness in terms of a conflict between internalized parental figures and infantile emotional needs (the superego, largely derived from early experiences of parental figures, and the id, made up of innate primitive impulses), invites its expression within the therapeutic relationship in this particular form. A social work agency, whose function is to provide a public service in respect of certain social problems, does not overtly invite people to express their problems to it in this way (though, of course, a worker within such an agency may, by the techniques he uses, eventually get his clients to express them in this form). Furthermore, the accepted theory assumes that the emotional content of the social work relationship (defined in terms of transference) is something quite different from the seeking of help with a social problem (seen as rational and realistic). It thus fails to recognize that a social work agency invites people to express themselves to it *in the form of* a social problem, and that therefore the emotional content of the relationship is to be found within the social problem presented and its manner of presentation.

I am not here trying to make a hard and fast distinction between neuroses and social problems, but rather pointing out the very obvious differences between the therapeutic structures of psychoanalytic clinics and social work agencies. While it is probably true that neurotic patients are more likely to experience their problems in terms of an internal conflict involving parental figures and emotional impulses, whereas people with social problems are more likely to be prone to behaviour which could be described as impulsive, immature or 'acting out', the differences between psychoanalysts and social workers are much greater and more readily identifiable than those between their clients. Social work theory, by trying to assimilate itself too closely with some aspects of psychoanalytic theory, has failed to give sufficient weight to these differences, and has thus risked misunderstanding what is happening in emotional terms between worker and client. The worker is seen as dealing with two different things, the emotional causes of the client's social problem, and the transference, which represents a resistance to his recognizing or accepting help with it. But if he is trying to look for these two separate aspects of the client's behaviour, he may well fail to recognize how both the social problem and the emotional content of the relationship are expressed within the way in which he and his client behave towards each other. Here is an example of a situation in which this is happening.

CASE EXAMPLE

A woman rings the social work agency to say that she wants to see someone urgently. She cannot come to the office, and it is extremely important that someone should visit her that evening. She is vague about the problem, which she would rather not discuss on the 'phone. She sounds desperate. A social worker visits her that evening. She tells him about a problem which comes broadly within the function of his agency. She is being evicted, or has debts, or her children are misbehaving. Something must be done about it. She is near to tears. She says she cannot go on any longer. The worker is struck by the vagueness of the problem, the fact that there is absolutely nothing that can be done about it that evening, and the very desperate state of mind of the client. He tries to convey to her his feeling that the problem cannot be solved by anything he can do on the spot. She starts to cry and to repeat that she is at her wits' end and cannot go on any more. Without mentioning suicide, she hints that there is only one other way out. When the worker tries to get her to say what it is that is upsetting her so much, she becomes even more tearful and less specific.

6

He begins to feel trapped, a prisoner to her half-spoken threat of suicide. He thinks of his other appointments, and wants to leave, but each time he tries to terminate the interview there is another outburst of desperation. The more he tries to get away, the more guilty he feels about it, and the less able he is to deal with the client's behaviour. He feels he cannot risk trying to get her to look at the threat of suicide, for fear that this will only make things worse. He hopes she will eventually calm down, but she does not. Finally he leaves, suddenly, apologetically, with her still crying and threatening. He is full of anxiety and guilt. Between his next two visits he tries to ring the Mental Welfare Officer, but cannot get through. He goes home and tells his wife all about it. That night he sleeps badly, wondering if he has walked out on somebody about to take her life. In the morning he visits her before going to work, and finds her looking quite different, perfectly healthy, and having quite obviously slept much better than he did.

In terms of the accepted theory, the client's problem appears to be closely connected with her inability to tolerate feelings of badness or depression within herself. She behaves towards the worker in a way which expresses great anxiety and dependence, and seems to invest him with a power to solve her problem in an immediate and magical way. She seems to expect him to behave in a way which will relieve her of her feelings of badness and depression instantaneously. The accepted theory would treat this as a transference phenomenon which goes with the rational request for help, consisting in a regression to a childish expectation of an omnipotent parental figure. It would try to distinguish these feelings from the 'real' problem. But in doing so it would miss the fact that this woman *succeeds* in making her approach to the agency in such a way that within a day the worker *does* carry away most of her bad feelings for her. The whole operation essentially consists in the client getting these feelings of badness and depression which she finds so intolerable outside herself and into the worker, so that she simply hands over this part of herself to him, and leaves him to do her worrying for her. Her emotional behaviour within the relationship is not so much an unrealistic outburst of infantile feelings as a means of accomplishing the purpose for which she originally demanded to see a social worker. The nature of her social problem, that she cannot contain her feelings of badness and depression within herself, is expressed in the relationship, in which she puts these feelings into the social worker, and gets him to act them out for her.

Defensive manoeuvres and transactions

According to the way of thinking I am suggesting, what happens between client and worker consists not so much of a request for help overlaid with emotional resistances as of a *defensive manoeuvre* by which the client protects herself against certain unwanted feelings about her situation. The manoeuvre serves the emotional purpose of relieving the client of these feelings by getting the worker to carry them for her, and is accomplished by means of the emotional behaviour which in the accepted theory is taken to be an expression of irrational resistance against help with the 'real' social problem. This behaviour enables the client to manipulate the worker into acting in a way which expresses those feelings which the client finds hardest to bear or to reconcile with her other feelings.

8

Social work agencies invite such defensive manoeuvres from their clients by offering help with social problems. This makes the worker a sort of recipient of those parts of people's personalities from which they feel most in need of escape at times of social crisis. I shall call the process by which this takes place the *transaction* between client and worker. The notion of a transaction in which the client gets the worker to act out unwanted parts of himself is not such a radical departure from psycho-analytic theory as it may seem. It is the proper equivalent in social work terms of the notions of transference and counter-transference, as I hope to show in the next chapter. The departure is rather from the accepted social work theory which creates a distinction between the problem which is brought to the agency and the trans-ference phenomenon. According to the way of thinking I am suggesting, the emotional transaction between client and worker is the expression of the social problem within these roles which corresponds to the transference expres-sion of the neurosis within the roles of patient and psychoanalyst.

I need now to give an actual example from a case of what I mean by a defensive manoeuvre and an emotional transaction between a client and a worker. The example I have chosen is of an apparently superficial contact between a casual caller at an agency and a worker who happened to be available when he arrived. It concerns a request for material help with a seemingly urgent immediate problem, the emotional significance of which was by no means obvious, but which emerged from sub-sequent events.

MR PETERSON

I have known Mr Peterson for nearly five years, and his circumstances have changed considerably, but the transaction that I want to illustrate occurred at our first meeting. He had been a tramp for about ten years, and was forty-seven years old. He had been in the armed services for some years, and on coming out had been married and soon divorced. After doing casual work in various parts of the country for many years, during which he served several prison sentences, he took to the road. He had been before the Courts about fifty times, and in recent years had often committed offences of malicious damage deliberately to get himself imprisoned. In Court he would point this out, saying that he had no home and was so desperate he had no choice but to commit an offence.

He was very well known in many offices of my agency, where he used to come and make aggressive demands for money. He had also made several token attempts at suicide, and had been in mental hospitals in connection with these.

He came in to my office one day demanding help. He was a man with a loud, aggressive voice, and he had been drinking. He told me he had been sleeping rough in the town, but there was nowhere for him to go and no work for him, so he had decided to move on. He was sure of work in the next town, but needed money for the bus fare. I asked how he could be sure of work there, but he told me not to worry about that. He said I had to realize that he was up against it. He couldn't go on living on nothing and sleeping out in the cold. If I just gave him the money he would be on his way, and I would not see him again.

Of course, I knew that Mr Peterson's story about the job was unrealistic. I knew that he would be no better off in the next town, and that he would probably go to my colleague there with exactly the same story. Equally, I knew that he was as likely to spend the money on drink as on his fare. However, he also made it plain that his desperation was real enough. Behind the aggressive demand for money there was a great despair about the hopelessness of his position which came across very clearly to me, and in the face of which I in turn felt helpless. I knew that there was no hope of finding him lodgings in the town in the condition he was in. I knew that there was no hostel nearby, and that in any case he hated hostels and would not stay in them. I felt that there was no contribution that I could make to help in the situation which faced Mr Peterson, and I was frightened of the feelings of depression and despair which I saw lying behind his anger. I felt unwilling to do anything that might provoke these feelings any further, and although giving him the money was obviously pointless, it seemed safer than refusing it and calling forth all the despair that motivated his request.

I gave him the money he asked for, and he went on his way. The following day he was in Court in the next town for an offence of malicious damage and sent to prison. When I heard of this I felt extremely guilty. I realized that what I had done was to run away from the feelings in Mr Peterson that I feared. He too had been trying to escape from these feelings by going to the next town, and had come presenting me with a request to provide this escape. I knew that it would not work, and he knew it, but I still colluded with his plan and gave him the money. It was a very rejecting thing to have done. He had promised to take himself and his intolerable problem out of my office for the sake of a bus fare, and I had been only too glad to get rid of him and it for that price. Once he had been confronted with the same feelings in the next town he had immediately committed another offence.

It was only in the light of subsequent events in my relationship with Mr Peterson that I realized the full significance of this first contact. Next time he came in with a very similar request, I steadily refused to give him money, at the same time offering him any other sort of help that it was in my power to give, and pointing out my awareness of his need for security and a home. His reaction was at first disbelief, then bitter sarcasm, and finally, as he saw I really meant it, explosive anger. He threatened to go out and commit a further offence at once, and stormed out. However, he later returned to apologize, and maintained his relationship with me until about a year afterwards, when he came back to me at a time when he was really determined to find himself somewhere to live. This he eventually achieved and he has now been living for over two years in his own flat. He is still in many ways a difficult person, but he is no longer a tramp.

During the period when he first came to me, Mr Peterson was using social workers like myself as part of a defensive manoeuvre in which he protected himself from feelings he could not bear. It was certainly no coincidence that he got into trouble the very day after I had given him the money. When Mr Peterson came in he was undoubtedly fighting the battle within himself between his feelings of depression and despair, and his wish to go on trying to make some sort of life in society outside prison.

The feelings of despair were threatening to overwhelm him, and he needed some sort of protection from them; the obvious answer was for him to escape into prison, but in order to be able to do this he had first to overcome his desires for a home and security within society, which were real, as subsequent events proved. To do this he came to me, a social worker whom he saw as standing for the community's wish for him to settle down and stop being a tramp. He handed over to me the side of his feelings that he felt I represented, the desire to get him settled down, and then threatened me with his despair, so that I was in as much jeopardy from it as he was. He threatened me in such a way as to offer an unrealistic escape from these feelings of his in the form of a request for money. If I could not stand the threat of his despair, then I would reject Mr Peterson by giving him the money, or by refusing it in a rejecting way. Either reaction would confirm that these feelings were unbearable for me, as they had been for Mr Peterson. The fact that I had to reject him in his despair proved to Mr Peterson that the community did not care, that society was against him. The giving of money was as big a rejection as the agency's withholding of it would have been. Both proved the same thing, and made it easier for Mr Peterson to commit his offence and get back into prison. Instead of having to battle with the part of himself that wanted to relate to other people in the community and to have the satisfactions of being a member of society, he put this part of himself into me, forced me to reject him, and thus proved to himself that nobody could stand him and his problem. When he got up in Court, Mr Peterson used to make a speech explaining this, saying that people like him were in a hopeless position, and nothing was being done for them. He even described his Court appearances as a campaign for better conditions for people like himself. By putting one part of himself into social workers like me, he could show himself that his prison sentences were not his failures but ours. By making us reject him, he made his breakdown partly our fault, and therefore easier to bear. His defensive manoeuvres consisted in getting the worker to act out the part of himself that found his failures so unbearable, and thus saved himself from having to live with it.

According to the way of thinking that I am putting forward, Mr Peterson's defensive manoeuvre resulted in a transaction in which he used me to carry part of his feelings, and to behave in a certain way towards him. It was not that he asked for help (realistic) in a way that provoked rejection (transference), but that he provoked rejection by someone into whom he had first put a part of himself that he could not bear to live with. The significance of the rejection lay in what the rejecting person represented of himself. Mr Peterson's expression of his emotional problem consisted in getting the 'anti-tramp' side of himself outside himself so he never had to face his need to relate to others and to be part of a community. He was able to do this by the way he used social workers, and it was not until this defensive manoeuvre was challenged that he could start to learn to live with this side of himself, and thus to change his way of life.

The analysis of Mr Peterson's defensive manoeuvre and his transaction with me is simplified by the fact that he was entirely alone in the world at the time. My other chief criticism of the accepted theory is that it tends to ignore the part played by the client's current pattern of social and family relationships in determining the form of his relationship with the worker and the role he gives the worker to play.

Transactions and the family

Although the accepted theory pays lip service to the importance of 'interaction' it is based on a concept of the individual personality which leaves little scope for factors arising in the client's other relationships to have any direct influence on the relationship between the client and the worker. Thus, Hollis (1964) suggests that theories of interaction are just another means of understanding the individual and the situation which he is in. Yet social work agencies invite clients to express themselves to their workers in terms of problems which concern their family or work relationships. Unlike the psychoanalyst who invites his patient to approach his problem as something within himself, the social worker is usually committed by the function of his agency to accepting clients' problems expressed in such a way that the client puts the problem outside himself.

In particular, social work in this country is increasingly concerned with problems arising from disturbances in family relationships, and in the maintenance of the family group. It seems important, therefore, to recognize the extent to which the relationship between client and worker is a function of the emotional dynamics of the family group from which the client comes.

My suggestion is that, just as an individual may get a social worker to carry his unwanted feelings for him, so a family may seek out a social worker and give him a role to play which corresponds to certain feelings which arise within the family, but which are feared to be incompatible with the various established roles within the family group. These established roles express an emotional *status quo* based on an unspoken agreement within the group about which feelings are most safely expressed by which members. Where a strong need arises for a particular feeling to be expressed by one or more members which runs counter to these roles, the fears aroused may lead the group to seek a social worker to act out these feelings for it. In this situation, all members of the group who have their reasons for fearing this role being acted out by a member of the family collude in giving this role to the social worker and forcing him to stay within this role.

THE CLARKE FAMILY

Here is an example of such a situation. Mr and Mrs Clarke approached me about the fact that two of their four children had on several occasions been involved in minor delinquencies and had been cautioned by the police. The parents described the boys, aged eleven and nine, as very irresponsible and difficult to control. They said they had made every effort to teach them to keep within the law without success, and they were now quite at a loss about the future, fearing that before long their boys would be before a Court. Mr and Mrs Clarke struck me as very sensible and concerned parents, anxious to do the right thing for their children.

When I saw the boys they were both very lively, rather cheeky, and quite demanding of my attention in a slightly aggressive way. They seemed to enjoy my visits, and wanted to make sure I came frequently. At the same time they expressed a good deal of contempt for the law and the authorities, and announced that they intended to continue to enjoy life in their own way.

In my interviews with Mr and Mrs Clarke, while I continued to find them co-operative and concerned about the boys, I was increasingly aware of tensions between them. Mr Clarke was a self-contained man whose main interest was in his stamp collection, over which he spent many solitary hours in the evening and at weekends. Mrs Clarke gradually expressed more and more resentment about the amount of time she was left on her own through this. Although she insisted that she 'hadn't thought of it before' she also acknowledged that her husband tended to leave the boys to their own devices. I began to feel that I was being used by the family to fulfil a paternal role towards the boys which Mr Clarke seemed to be evading. When I tried to put this to him he insisted, evidently sincerely, that he was very fond of the boys, but that it was very important to him to have an absorbing hobby such as his stamp collection. When I tried to cut down on my visits to the boys, there was strong resistance both from them and from the parents. I therefore continued to see the boys regularly, but to concentrate my attention increasingly on the relationship between Mr and Mrs Clarke.

Before long it became plain that Mr Clarke had a great deal of anxiety about his role as a husband. He feared the emotional and even the sexual demands that his wife might make on him, and used his stamp collection as a defence in which he took refuge from her. Mrs Clarke had been inwardly very resentful about this, but powerless to do anything about it. She herself had had an aggressive father who had terrorized her mother, and her greatest fear was of having a husband who would behave in the same way. She therefore subtly colluded with her husband's passive withdrawal which seemed preferable to the dangers of the opposite extreme. All her resentment about being neglected by him was acted out by her sons, also with her unconscious collusion or even encouragement. On the other hand, while their behaviour was partly attention seeking, they did not really want their father to play a part in controlling them, preferring the less effective attentions of an outsider like myself. Although Mr and Mrs Clarke felt guilty and confused about their failure to be satisfactory parents to their children, they could neither of them allow Mr Clarke to take the role of an effective father because of their shared fears about the implications of this role. They therefore used me in the role of a paternal and controlling figure for the boys.

In working with Mr and Mrs Clarke over quite a long period it was possible to help them express and come to terms with their fears. Mr Clarke's doubts about the role of husband and father were based partly on anxieties about his own masculinity and partly on the realistic observation of his wife's need to dominate him and prevent him from asserting himself in their relationship or his relationship with the children. She was ultimately able to recognize this and some of her reasons for behaving in this way, and their relationship began to improve steadily, while Mr Clarke's stamp collection became much less important. Ultimately they both began to play a much more active part in controlling the boys, and more able to allow me to withdraw from the situation altogether.

In this case the role given to me by the family was quite a 'good' one, based on the need for a positive, concerned and reasonably controlling person to take charge of the two boys. This role corresponded with the part which Mr Clarke was quite capable of playing in the family, but from which he had by tacit consent been excluded and excluded himself. Their reasons for handing it over to me were not connected with the 'bad' implications of being a punishing or controlling person in the general sense, but with the particular private implications for the family group of allowing Mr Clarke to fulfil this role. Once their fears had been dealt with the family no longer needed a social worker to do this for them.

With the family group as with the individual, much of the emotional behaviour taken in the accepted theory as an expression of transference resistance to help with the problem in hand can be seen as defensive manipulation of the worker into the required role. The Clarke boys' aggressive attention seeking as much as their father's anxious evasion forced me for a time to carry the feelings that they feared and to play the role from which Mr Clarke was being excluded. What was happening was a process of getting these feelings to be expressed outside the group and not within it, which constituted the group's transaction with me.

I am therefore concerned in this book to look at the processes by which individuals and groups can get emotions outside themselves and into social workers. It seems to me that such processes have been largely ignored, and that they require understanding because they are characteristic of relationships between people with social problems and the people to whom they turn for help.

To understand these processes, I need first to look at what is known in general terms about how people get feelings outside themselves and into other people, and the distribution of feelings within groups. This is the subject of my next chapter.

2

The inner world and the transmission of feelings

If one person gets another to act out a part of himself, he must be disowning that part. For him to get it outside himself and into someone else he must want not to have it within himself. He must want not to own it.

Historically, any study of the disowned parts of the self must start with Freud and his notion of the unconscious. He saw in the symptoms of neurotic patients, in dreams and phantasies and slips of the tongue indications of a part of people's psychic structure of which they were unaware, and which they were very reluctant to recognize. Freud analysed this part of the psyche in terms of a pool of instincts which were innate, timeless, impersonal, existing without reference to external realities and unmodified by experience. He saw these instincts as fundamentally antisocial, which explained how they came to be repressed during childhood in accordance with the demands of life in a civilized society.

Later psychoanalysts, and especially those of the school of Melanie Klein, have analysed the disowned part of the self in terms of a splitting off from the original self of certain early experiences of relations with the outside world, and particularly of relations with parental figures. In their theories, very early experiences, especially unsatisfactory ones with the mother figure, come to be split off from the self and internalized, but relegated to an inner world. This inner world is seen as interacting more freely with the outer world of everyday experience than the original unconscious of Freud's theory, but is still evidenced principally only in the disguised form of dreams, phantasies and symptoms.

It is important to recognize that these theories about the disowned parts of the self were developed primarily to explain the symptoms of neurotic and psychotic patients, and particularly their apparent dissociation from parts of their feelings and personalities whose existence was clearly indicated by their dreams and phantasies and by some of their behaviour. It was, therefore, natural for such theories to think of the disowned parts of the personality as stored 'within' the self, as an 'inner' world, and to look for them by a process of 'deep' psychoanalysis.

*The Family Discussion Bureau's theory**

What happens when this way of thinking is applied to the study of the way in which people behave towards each other? The Family Discussion Bureau have looked at marital interaction from the standpoint of Kleinian theory, and have used this to develop an analysis of how people's behaviour towards each other is related to their inner

* The Family Discussion Bureau is now known as The Institute of Marital Studies, but the publications referred to in this section appeared under the old name.

worlds. They make particular use of the concepts of 'projection' and 'introjection'. In their definition

> ... we understand by introjection that situations lived through, and objects encountered by the subject, are not only experienced as external, but are taken into the self to become part of a continuing inner life, and by projection that feelings and ideas that come from inside can be attributed to people and objects outside. (Pincus and Bannister, 1965).

To account for the way in which a couple's feelings and behaviour so often fit together into a complementary pattern, they rely on explanations in terms of the partners' inner worlds, derived from introjected childhood experiences with parental figures. Because, as they suggest, 'strong unconscious ties to first love objects may help to determine the choice of a partner with whom the earlier situation can be compulsively re-enacted', each partner's hidden inner phantasies about himself and the other tend to be confirmed and reinforced by the other's behaviour and by his own (Pincus, 1962). Each chooses a partner whose behaviour confirms his inner world of phantasy, and in turn behaves in a way which confirms his partner's.

The question which I find it difficult to answer from the writings of the Family Discussion Bureau is: within a relationship, where does the inner world of phantasy end, and the outer 'real' world of the relationship begin? It is one thing to say that the reality of the relationship tends to confirm the inner phantasy, or to play into it, but to what extent is one person's behaviour influenced or affected by the 'inner world' of the other? Is it just that certain parts of the one partner's self are inwardly *attributed* to the other, or is it that they outwardly enter into the relationship so as to have an effect on the other's behaviour?

Certain passages from the work of the Family Discussion Bureau suggest that they see the disowned parts of the personality as entering directly into marital relationships, so that one partner's behaviour is directly influenced by his having to carry the disowned feelings of the other. For instance:

> ... in marital work, the unrecognized or unconscious aspect of a client's personality is often revealed in the partner. This offers the caseworker an opportunity to help husband and wife to recognize in each other these hitherto disowned parts of themselves which often represent the very opposite of those aspects of their personalities which are most accepted and of which they are aware. ... The therapeutic effectiveness of marital work lies in the possibility of helping each partner to recognize, as a step on the difficult road to accepting and tolerating them, the denied or rejected parts of themselves, which they have found in or projected on to their partner. ... The person who complains of his partner's depression, dependence, or dominance may well, by denying his own, leave the partner to express a double dose. ... (Pincus, 1962.)

> The rejected parts still have to be dealt with, now outside oneself, but ever present. ... The more at war with himself an individual is, the more of himself he may project, and the more dependent he may become on the container of his projections. (Pincus and Bannister, 1965.)

The notion which I find particularly important here is that of the 'double dose'. It implies that one partner's behaviour and feelings are intensified and exaggerated by the direct influence of the other partner, by means of the part of the other that is being denied or disowned. This means that one person is in some sense carrying or acting out feelings which belong to another, in the sense that they arise within that other person, but are denied or disowned by him in such a way as to put them into the first person.

This way of thinking about relationships has been widely accepted by social workers as applying not only to the marital relationship but also to other family relationships. The notion that one person may carry part of the feelings of another member of his family can help to explain many kinds of behaviour difficulties within the family. It can assist in the explanation of delinquency and other problematic behaviour by children. In the first chapter I introduced the Clarke family as an example of how certain feelings were carried by different members of the family group. In this family, the two boys tended to act out their mother's rebellion against what she felt to be her neglect by her husband, and this was a partial explanation of much of their difficult behaviour.

In the field of mental illness a similar concept has proved of value. Although the theoretical background to their work is entirely different, Laing and his associates (1964) have shown that the parents they studied make a major unconscious contribution to the behaviour of schizophrenics.

My suggestion is that this way of thinking is of particular value to social workers because they are primarily concerned with the relationships between people rather than the relationships between different parts of an individual's personality. Because people who come to social work agencies are invited by the function of the agency to present their problems in terms of their relationships both in and outside the family, a theory which can account for the way in which people put parts of themselves outside themselves is especially valuable. However, this way of thinking has tended to be used in a piecemeal way alongside, or superimposed upon, other theories, and it has not always been fully developed, particularly in its application to the relationship between client and worker. It seems to me that this is partly because the theoretical implications of the notion of the 'double dose' have not been sufficiently examined.

It is obviously impossible within the scope of this book to look at all these implications, but the one that I am most concerned with here is how the concept of the 'double dose' is related to that of 'projection'. The Family Discussion Bureau's way of thinking is based on an orthodox Kleinian view of the individual's personality, and because of this there is an ambiguity, to which I have already drawn attention, about the relationship between the inner world and external reality. If projection is the mechanism which carries the double dose, how can it simply consist in a person attributing a part of his inner world to another? To attribute in phantasy an inner part of the self to another person could not lead directly to that person's behaviour being influenced in any way. If disowned parts of the self were confined to an inner world and only attributed to others, how could they enter directly into a relationship to the extent of exaggerating or intensifying another person's behaviour or feelings?

A question arises, therefore, as to whether it is really appropriate to think of disowned parts of the self as belonging only to a private inner world, or instead to think of them as the kind of things that can enter directly

25

into a relationship, so that the disowned parts of one person can influence the behaviour of another. Is such a notion, which would clearly involve a process of unconscious communication between people, absurd? Could the disowned parts of one person, of which he was unaware, be expressed or acted out by another person on his behalf?

The notion of personality structure

To some extent, the question of whether or not such a notion makes sense must depend on how we think of the disowned 'parts' of the personality to which we refer. If we think in terms of Freud's original theory, it would plainly be absurd to suppose that a person's innate biological drives could be found anywhere but inside him. Equally, a person's internalized experiences of the first year of life could not enter directly into his current relationships. If by a disowned 'part' of a person we mean a part of the 'structure' of his personality, then it is plain that such a part could not be anywhere but 'inside' him.

However, the notion of a personality *structure*, while it has always been part of the Freudian and Kleinian way of thinking, is no longer acceptable in philosophical theories of personality or in the theories of experimental psychology. Ryle (1949) pointed out that when we talk of a person's personality we mean the way he can be expected to behave in certain situations. We do not imply anything about a structure inside him, nor is there any logical reason to suppose such a structure exists. Experimental psychologists have analysed behaviour in terms of conditioned responses to experiences in the environment. The process of conditioning in childhood gives rise not to an internal structure but to the pattern of an individual's continuous responses to the external world, the perception of which constitutes our knowledge of his personality.

I am certainly not going to suggest that people do not have an inner world of which they are unaware. I am simply suggesting that it is misleading to think of this in terms of a permanent structure, constructed either out of instincts or of internalized experiences, built up within the mind as part of something like a large machine. Once we reject the notion of a permanent structure it becomes possible to think of the disowned parts of the personality in a very different way.

If we accept the idea from experimental psychology that a person's experiences, starting from birth, teach him to reproduce some responses to his environment and to inhibit others, then it remains an open question what happens to his impulses towards the responses which he has learnt to inhibit. Because a person learns at a very early age not to react by violent anger when he is frustrated, it does not mean that similar frustration in later life does not impel him to anger. But nor does it necessarily mean that such an experience calls up from within him a secret store of infantile anger that has been part of his inner world ever since. It means simply that he deals with this impulse to anger in the way which he learnt to deal with it in childhood. This is not necessarily to store it away, or to confine it within himself. It may well be 'to give' it to somebody else.

Since the process which experimental psychologists call conditioning takes place within a period when the child is part of a family group it is logical to suppose the child learns which emotional responses to reproduce (express) and which to inhibit (disown) as part of the emotional

27

pattern of responses of his family. My suggestion is simply that the child's pattern of responses that we call his personality is learnt in relation to this, and that those emotions which he comes to disown can just as reasonably be supposed to be put into other members of the group as kept within himself. Within the pattern of these relationships he may well deal with some emotions in one way, and with others in the other. In fact, it may be even more complicated than this. In his relationship with his mother he may be able to express anger, in that with his father he may disown it and internalize it; and in that with his brother he may disown it but get his brother to act it out on his behalf. Thus, the same emotion could be dealt with in three different ways by one child in his earliest family relationships.

This way of thinking requires that we should think of the disowned parts of the self as emotional responses to situations prevented from reaching consciousness in accordance with a pattern resulting from childhood experiences of relationships. Some of these early experiences, I suggest, consist in the child discovering that within his family group, while it is unsafe for him to express certain emotions, there is another member of the family who can express and act them out for him. This gives rise to the possibility of an unconscious response to a situation being communicated from one person to another who is emotionally involved in the same situation. Once this kind of relationship is experienced in early life in respect of certain emotions it can give rise in later life to a need for a new person to accept that part of the self which is being disowned, so that he can express it for him.

This last notion goes beyond those that I have quoted of the Family Discussion Bureau in two ways. In the first place it implies that the disowned parts of one person which are involved in a relationship of this kind are not parts of that person's inner world which are attributed by projection to the other person, but emotional reactions which, by means of an unconscious process of communication between them, come to be acted out by the other person on his behalf. Secondly, it implies that this can occur not only in the marital relationship, but in any relationship where one person has a need to disown part of his feelings and put them into somebody else, and where there is another person who shares his situation emotionally and is in a position unconsciously to accept and express these feelings. For instance, where a person cannot get a member of his family group to accept a feeling about his situation that he has a need to disown, he may turn to somebody outside the family. Very often a social worker provides for this need by his willingness to share the emotional situation and to accept the unwanted feelings. Although the process of unconscious communication to which I have referred occurs most commonly within family groups, I shall try to explain and illustrate it from the relationship between client and social worker, as this is the focus of this book.

Transference and countertransference

I have already suggested in the first chapter that there is a closer correspondence between the way of thinking I am putting forward about client-worker transactions and the psychoanalytic notions of transference and countertransference than there is between the latter and the accepted theory of the social work relationship. Recently, psychoanalysts have paid increasing attention to countertransference phenomena, not merely from the point of view of understanding the analyst's irrational feelings about the patient, but also to explain the analyst's ability to relate directly to the unconscious of the patient. Racker (1968) suggests that a skilled and sensitive analyst identifies the whole of his personality with that of his patient, so that each part of his personality relates directly with the corresponding part of the patient's. These identifications are

> ... based on introjection and projection, or, in other terms, on the resonance of the exterior in the interior, on recognition of what belongs to another as one's own ('this part of you is I') and on the equation of what is one's own with what belongs to another ('this part of me is you').

A further set of identifications

> ... are produced by the fact that the patient treats the analyst as an internal (projected) object, and in consequence the analyst feels treated as such; that is, he identifies himself with this object.

Here are two quotations which illustrate the sort of phenomena to which Racker refers:

> ... at times the analyst—if his unconscious is well connected with that of the patient—may perceive her repressed or split-off sexual excitement through sexual sensations of his own, in a certain way 'induced' by the patient.

> Violent irruptions of countertransference anxiety occur at times—as I have already mentioned—as a consequence of the analyst's identification with violently threatened, or attacked, or with seriously worried or

'guilty' internal objects, or else as a consequence of his identification with parts of the patient's ego which are intensely split off and 'projected' on to the analyst.

What we seem to have in these quotations is a picture of an analyst and a patient whose inner worlds are in communication with each other by some process other than the normal means of conscious communication between people. What is this process? Racker links it with notions of projection and introjection, but he does not define these any differently from Klein or from the Family Discussion Bureau. And yet his way of thinking clearly implies some unconscious emotional 'inner eye' by which the analyst unconsciously perceives the disowned parts of the patient. Thus, for instance his own sexual feelings are intensified by those of the patient, which are being disowned, by means of this unconscious internal perception, based on introjection and projection, which allows him to feel her feelings as well as his own.

This process corresponds exactly with the one I am suggesting takes place between the client and the social worker. The worker acts out a disowned part of the client's personality because the client succeeds in getting him to experience a 'double dose' of the feelings that correspond to the ones she is denying. The phenomena that Racker analyses in terms of countertransference will be very familiar to most social workers.

However, I do not find Racker's analysis of these phenomena in terms of projection and introjection convincing when applied to the relationship between a social worker and his client. He bases it upon the notion of a therapeutic identification of a kind which, though clearly applicable to the psychoanalytic situation, does not correspond with that of social work. The social worker does not often invite his client to express his problems in terms of internal conflicts nor does he attempt to identify himself with the conflicting parts of the client's personality. He invites the client to express himself in the form of a social problem, and he tries to play a role within the client's social situation.

I have already suggested that the way in which some people use social workers to carry their disowned feelings for them can in part be accounted for in terms of early experiences within the family group of using other members of the family to carry such feelings. This way of dealing with a feeling that is disowned is different from the way which consists in confining it 'within' the child. Where in adult life a person experiences a situation in which he feels a need to deal with a similar feeling in this way, he may turn to a social worker, particularly if there is no one in his current family group who can safely carry this feeling. Provided that he can, by a defensive manoeuvre of the kind I have illustrated in the first chapter, involve the worker emotionally in his situation, he may be able to get the worker to accept the disowned part of himself, and so deal with it according to the pattern he learnt in childhood.

The transmission of feelings

Such a process is evidently very different from the Kleinian notion of projection, which consists in a person attributing part of his inner world to another. It seems to me that it is misleading to call this process by the same name, and I have suggested elsewhere (1968) that it should be distinguished from projection by the term 'transmission'. A person transmits a feeling when he succeeds in getting it right outside himself and into another person, who experiences a double dose of that feeling, consisting of his own feeling reinforced by that which is transmitted from the first person.

Thus the phenomena in social work which correspond to those to which Racker draws attention in psychoanalysis need not be explained by recourse to the notion of an unconscious emotional 'inner eye' through which the worker perceives and acts out feelings in the client which remain part of the client's internal personality structure. They can be accounted for by the worker's involvement in the client's emotional situation, his acceptance, often as a result of the client's defensive manoeuvre, of the role and feelings that the client requires of him, and the double dose of feelings experienced as a result of the process of transmission of feelings from the client.

However, this form of analysis could be criticized as dealing superficially with the relation between the client's early experiences within his family group and his later relationships, including that between him and the worker. In stating simply that the client reproduces a way of dealing with a part of himself which he has learnt within his family group, it seems to be doing less than justice to the complexity both of his early relationships and his relationship with the worker. It has none of the richness of Kleinian object relations theory, which constructs in such detail an inner world of infantile experiences with which the later exterior realities of adult relationships can interact. However, as I shall try to illustrate from an example there is no reason why the way of thinking that I am putting forward should not be similarly detailed in elaborating the relations between early experiences and current realities. The difference is that according to my way of thinking these early relationships constitute the learning experience by which the later patterns of emotional reactions are determined rather than an inner world which forms part of a personality structure having a permanent 'existence' within the self.

JAMES

The example I have chosen is of James, aged nineteen, who came under my supervision as a result of a court appearance for possessing cannabis resin and amphetamine pills. He came from a working-class family, and his father, who died when he was fourteen years old, had done a manual job. James had been to Grammar School, but told me that he did not enjoy it, and had chosen to leave when he was fifteen, before taking G.C.E., to get a job as an apprentice in a factory. On completing his apprenticeship he had left home for six months to live a bohemian life with a group of friends in London and elsewhere, doing casual work. He had now been sent home by the court on a condition of residence. He gave the impression of being a fairly typical representative of his group, articulate, with many ideas about social reform and the evils of the consumer society. He acknowledged that he and his friends were rebellious 'in a quiet sort of way', but felt that the legalization of soft drugs would solve most of their problems. He hated the idea of being home, and said that he would be bored to tears in a very short time. When I suggested that eighteen years of family background and upbringing must have made some mark on him and left him with some common ground with neighbours and family, he strongly denied this, saying he had much more in common with

34

his present friends and the people he had met in London.

In the first four interviews his attitude towards me was one of amused tolerance which seemed somewhat assumed and which evidently concealed quite a lot of anxiety. There was no hostility in it, though I felt that he was partly disappointed that I refused to argue with him over the general issue of the merits of soft drug legalization. James was out of work at this time, and when in the next interview we started to discuss this I noticed a new factor in our relationship which was hard to define. He seemed to be much more willing to show me his vulnerability and sense of failure in this sphere than in other matters, where he put across an impression of self-sufficiency and independence which was not convincing. Over the question of work he admitted that he did not know the answer. He had a vague interest in working with people, and regretted lacking qualifications for a job which would allow him to follow this up. He despised the world of industry and commerce in which he felt that people were mere machines and less than human. The trade that he had learnt condemned him to be like this if he stayed in it. He thought that the whole establishment in the consumer society was trying to condition people to accept this kind of existence. When I asked him if he included social workers in the establishment, he said he thought not. He felt social workers had found their own personal answer to the dilemma of a choice between faceless conformity or opting out. When I pointed out that this solution was mere escapism unless they could really help others to find their own solution too, and that this could not reasonably take the form of turning everyone else into a social worker as well, James seemed not to have thought of this. He talked about his lack of confidence in his ability to do a

35

job that required genuine originality, initiative or creativity for some time at the end of this interview.

About a month later James got a job, not in his trade but also in a factory, on repetitive production work. He explained to me that he was taking it only to save money, as he was planning to go abroad when his condition of residence ended. Soon he began to come into conflict with the police again, being arrested on two occasions on suspicion of possessing drugs, but in each case no charge was eventually made. Not long afterwards he came to me with a wild story about the police following him and watching his house. He seemed aware of how unrealistic he was being, and even talked of 'paranoia', but he was obviously genuinely frightened. Next time I saw him he was calmer, and I took up with him his perpetual conflict with the police and his feelings of persecution in terms of a conflict within himself between different parts of his personality, saying I felt that there was part of himself which could be identified with the police. This he laughingly denied.

Three months after taking this job, he began to complain about how dull it was, and say that he was depressed. I pointed out his apparently deliberate choice, both in his apprenticeship and his present job, of repetitive work which made him like a robot. There seemed to be nothing for him but a choice between this or the aimlessness of a bohemian existence outside the normal community. In talking about alternative ways of life, James became less articulate, more depressed and increasingly drew attention to his 'lack of confidence'. He mentioned an interest in mental nursing, asked me to tell him about it, but did nothing himself to follow it up. On the other hand he had his hair cut quite short, and came in to see me looking more tidily dressed than before. I began to feel very guilty about the fact that I was doing nothing practical to help James out of his dilemma. I thought in terms of enquiring after jobs on his behalf, and did actually ring up a mental hospital. Gradually I became aware that James was putting these feelings into me through the way he behaved and doing nothing himself towards finding a solution of his problem. My guilt and the impulse to get him all fixed up with a nice job seemed to be the result of a defensive manoeuvre on his part to protect himself from having to face the side of his personality which represented the very opposite of his anxious lack of confidence, and required him to assert himself.

Eventually, when James was talking one day about his 'lack of vocation', I put it to him that he seemed to be asking me to put him in a job of my choice. I suggested that this might possibly be because he had lost his father at a time when he might have looked to him for guidance in the matter of a career. James at once confirmed this very readily, and went on to say that his father certainly would not have let him leave school without his G.C.E. His father had always been ambitious for him, and had made him go to the Grammar School rather against his will. He had always had his father to push him up to the age of fourteen, and his death had undoubtedly been the reason for his taking the apprenticeship rather than staying on at school to get qualifications.

After this James remained rather depressed and anxious, but he seemed to be making a great effort to come to terms with himself. He began to acknowledge that his fears about the police, his suspicions and his lack of confidence were all connected with the fact that he had, in taking drugs, gone right against the standards by which he had

had been brought up, and particularly those of his father. He could acknowledge directly not only that his feelings about the police were a reflection of his own guilt, but also that the family standards that he had broken were as much a part of him as of them. He was also much troubled about feeling unacceptable and boring, being convinced that he could not find a place for himself in the community outside his depressing factory because he was such a dull and inarticulate person. I contrasted this attitude with those he had first expressed when he came to see me, pointing out how full of ideas he had been then. James smilingly but guiltily told me that on those occasions he had taken several stimulant pills before coming to my office. He said that this was just part of the mad escapist mood in which he had lived at that time.

By now James also recognized his dependence on the mechanical job he was doing and no longer rationalized his choice entirely in terms of financial benefits. He wanted to find another kind of life, but mistrusted his previous escapism and his former friends. He told me that he now saw this behaviour as a way of trying to pretend to himself that he could do anything he wanted to by avoiding actually doing anything. One day he came to see me in a mood of particular anxiety about the rut he felt himself to be in. He said that the only time when he could recognize a more positive and assertive side of himself had been when he was taking amphetamine pills, and he wondered whether he could get these on prescription from a doctor. He was aware that he might be asking something unrealistic, but he seemed genuinely anxious for an answer. I agreed to think about what he was asking, and to discuss it with him when I next saw him.

This request was obviously an attempt to involve me in

some direct interaction between his conflicting emotions but I was not at all sure of its full significance. For a defensive manoeuvre it was a particularly overt and direct piece of manipulation and at a time when James had known me for over a year, and had come to understand the sort of way I reacted to him. I decided to put to James the kind of way that he and I had come to understand his actions to see whether it was possible in this context to get a better grasp of what he was asking.

When I saw him I told him this, and set out the position as I saw it. Firstly, it seemed that James had tended to react to me as someone he could use in the sort of role that his father had played towards him during his childhood. He seemed to have the feeling that I could give the push he needed to establish a more satisfactory way of life. However, I had felt that he had now accepted that because I was not his father I could not play this role satisfactorily, and that in any case he was unlikely in the long run to accept someone else's choice for his life. On the other hand, he seemed when on his own and away from home to have found in drugs a means to the assertiveness and initiative that he felt were lacking in him. For him drugs seemed to represent potency of a kind, and not to have them represented a loss of potency. But on the other hand, the taking of drugs ran against his whole upbringing and family standards, so he felt very guilty about taking them. (At this point James, who had been acknowledging these suggestions, added that amphetamine taking also went contrary to the standards of many of his former friends, so he received little support from them.) These guilt feelings were displaced on to policemen by whom James felt persecuted. So how were we to understand his present request? He seemed to look to me as if to a father to help him be assertive and potent in a legal way. James took this further to suggest that in asking for drugs on prescription he was seeking the only form of potency he knew, but doing this in a legal way, and if possible with my permission. This sounded very persuasive. I suggested that it was not the drugs themselves that were his potency, but only that they represented it to him. James still felt he needed them, and he seemed to put me in a position where if I did not support him in this I would either be condemning him to perpetual depression or to seeking illegal means of getting drugs. We discussed the whole thing further for a time, before I agreed that if he would get an appointment with a psychiatrist I would accompany him there and discuss his request with him.

During the weeks that he was waiting for this appointment, James's depression lifted. He became much more positive, and found himself a girlfriend, whom he brought in to introduce to me. When we eventually went to the psychiatrist, however, he presented himself as utterly depressed and inarticulate. I found myself put in the position of arguing his case for him because he did it so badly himself. The psychiatrist had no hesitation in turning down the request, pointing out that James was obviously depressed and that amphetamines were now regarded as an unsatisfactory form of treatment for depression. It also became clear from what he said that James intended to use these drugs to stimulate himself for certain kinds of activities, mainly social, and not as a means towards altering his whole way of life.

James was angry at being turned down, but I pointed out quite strongly to him afterwards how successfully he had used me in this whole operation, which in the end boiled down to his finding a means of enjoying himself at parties. I suggested that what he really needed was to come to terms with the considerable potential for initiative and self-assertion which he quite obviously had in him, and of which this whole exercise had been good evidence. After that I saw James only twice more. He went off with his girlfriend, finally breaking out of the rut in which he had felt himself imprisoned long after his residence order expired. When I last heard from him he was living and working in a large city.

What I think this example shows is the very different ways in which a person can in his early family experiences learn to deal with different feelings. Partly because of the position I occupied in relation to him as a social worker, but also because of his needs in his current family situation, he behaved to me in terms of these feelings according to the pattern he had established early in life in his relationship with his father. After his early testing out to see what sort of a person I was (in which his anxieties and fears were masked by his drug taking) he quickly settled upon using me to carry the disowned assertive part of himself so that I could play a role similar to that taken by his father. As a small boy he had clearly been dominated by a father who was very ambitious for him and anxious that he should follow the way of life he had chosen for him. Within this relationship James could not assert himself, and he disowned his own assertiveness by letting his father express it for him. Such a relationship must have aroused a good deal of anger in James as a child, but once again he felt unsafe to express it in relation to his dominant father, and guilty about it too. This anger was displaced on to the bad father figures, like teachers and ultimately policeman, whom he saw as persecuting him in an exaggerated version of his own father's behaviour. Whereas he transmitted his assertiveness to his father, and eventually to me, he projected his anger on to policemen by quite a different process. In the case of his depression, this feeling was dealt with in yet another way. James seems to have experienced depression not only for himself but for his father also. He identified himself with this feeling, and ultimately with all the depressive aspects of his father's life. When his father died he immediately chose, not to take on the assertive dominant role in the family, but to follow an occupation similar to his father's, and from which his father was trying to help him escape. Perhaps he not only introjected the depressive parts of his father's position; he may also have carried a double dose of depression transmitted from his father during his life, and also a similar double dose from me about my inability to help him change during his period under my supervision.

It was the conflict between all these feelings in relation to father figures that James acted out with me during the time I knew him. His experiences in childhood had established a way of dealing with his emotions which brought him to the position of a person who had opted out of life in the community and who depended on drugs for the satisfaction of his needs. In his relationship with me the full and complex nature of the social problem was expressed and worked through according to the pattern established between him and his father. It is thus that I am suggesting the client-worker transaction is related to the client's early experiences of relationships.

3
Social work with disruptive people

The doctor-patient game

I have suggested that some people are able to use their relationship with a social worker as a means of getting a disowned part of themselves to be carried by the worker. This way of thinking implies that a client can influence the worker's behaviour through disowned feelings which may be strong, primitive and irrational. If this way of thinking has any validity, how does it affect the analysis of the ways in which social workers can help their clients to deal with their social problems?

It is part of the accepted theory of the social work relationship that the helping role of the worker towards the client is similar to the role of a doctor towards his patient. In spite of all that has been written by casework theorists to distinguish between the work done by medically trained psychotherapists and that done by caseworkers, there are obvious similarities in their descriptions of the aims and methods of the two professions. The language of casework theory—of 'diagnosis' and 'treatment'—indicates this well enough. In describing the results of one piece of casework treatment, Hollis (1964) writes that there was

> ... a generally greater forcefulness of ego functioning that comes with more self-confidence and freedom from tension and anxiety (comparable to the better functioning of the body when it is free from fatigue and tension).

There are certain important consequences of this view of the social worker's helping role. If a client's faulty social functioning is seen as similar to a fault in the functioning of his body, then this puts him in the same sort of position in relation to the social worker as he would be as a patient to his doctor. The worker's first task must be to find out what is wrong with the client, and it is assumed that this will become apparent by asking the client to tell him about it. The client is seen as taking part in an activity which is aimed at putting right what is wrong with him. Once this is understood, it makes sense to expect the client to behave in a certain way consistent with the role of somebody who has something wrong with him going to see somebody who is there to put it right. It is clear that he should tell the worker about his symptoms, and co-operate in whatever treatment the worker decides upon by keeping appointments and discussing his problems.

Unfortunately, some clients do not easily accept this role. They refuse to play the doctor-patient game. They do not seem to recognize the worker as someone who is there to help them correct their faulty social functioning. They do not give him all the information he needs for his diagnosis. They do not keep appointments. They come in at all sorts of odd times with a bewildering variety of social crises, and their own unrealistic solutions to them. They are said to be 'impulsive' or 'immature', to be suffering from 'behaviour disorders', to be prone to 'acting out'. Their actions are accounted for either in terms of the very severe stresses of environmental difficulties or of their lack of 'ego-strength' to deal with their unruly emotions. Because they form a fairly large proportion of most social workers' caseloads, casework theorists have tried hard to suggest constructive ways of dealing with them, but on the whole they tend to issue warnings about the dangers of over-ambitious attempts to help such people. Discussing the choice of treatment procedures, and dealing only with educational and cultural factors, Hollis (1964) warns that

> ... as a result of these environmental factors, which cannot always be adequately cleared away, very few under-educated, economically hard-pressed individuals have been brought to the point of readiness for inward understanding.

Emotional factors are even more limiting, and she writes that 'very rarely would a person experiencing extreme anxiety be able to deal constructively with any extensive inner exploration'.

I believe that such under-educated, economically hard-pressed, impulsive, anxious people can provide many clues about what is wrong with the doctor-patient way of thinking about the social work relationship. By refusing to play the game according to the rules of casework theory, they indicate the weaknesses of these rules. The biggest weakness is that the game is formulated in such a way that it often seems as if only the social worker has aims and plans and things he is trying to do to the client. It fails to take account of the things that the client is trying to do to him. It is like describing the game of cricket purely from the bowler's point of view, acknowledging that the batsman may do things that make it difficult to get him out (the client may have resistances against treatment) but failing to recognize that the batsman is aiming to make runs off the bowler.

The point about people like this is not just that it is difficult to do to them the sort of things that social workers are supposed to do, but that they get us to feel and do things which are not comfortable for us. It is not simply the difficulty of having an effect on their behaviour and feelings, but of their effect on ours. They make us feel very angry or very frightened, very protective or very rejecting. They get us to give them frequent material help, or they repeatedly engineer their admission to institutions. If we try to ignore these feelings or to rationalize these actions we are failing to understand what our relationship with such people is all about, because they are an essential part of this relationship. If casework theory fails to recognize that some people come to agencies with such covert aims as to seek rejection, to browbeat the worker, or imprison him, or scare him out of his wits, then it can provide the worker with little guidance as to how such people can be helped.

This difficulty really stems from a way of thinking which sees everything that the worker does in terms of treatment and everything the client does in terms of symptoms. Because there are two different languages for describing the behaviour of the two parties it is impossible to analyse the transaction which takes place between them. Thus, for instance, Hollis (1964) warns of psychotic or near-psychotic clients who might start to produce increasingly bizarre material, and who should therefore be encouraged not to dwell on such matters too much. It is assumed that this avoidance of bizarre material by the worker is for the client's good rather than because the worker finds such phantasies frightening. It is also assumed that these phantasies are a symptom of illness rather than a means of influencing the worker's behaviour, or testing him out. It ignores the possibility that the client may be aware that his phantasies are frightening for other people, and in particular for the worker. It assumes that there is an objective distinction between material which is bizarre and psychotic and material which is not. Who can be absolutely sure that he can tell the difference between a psychotic person and someone who is simply scaring us, or even that there is a difference?

According to the way of thinking which Hollis represents a person who behaves in this sort of way is showing that his ego is not functioning sufficiently well to keep under control certain irrational and potentially dangerous impulses. According to the way of thinking I am suggesting it is the worker's ego rather than the client's that may be under threat. Because the client is able to influence the worker's feelings and behaviour by means of the transmission of disowned parts of his personality, the worker may find himself troubled by ideas and feelings which run counter to his standards of professional behaviour. To be annoyed or bored or frightened by a client is disturbing because of the worker's principles of acceptance and his desire to be helpful and positive. Such people make it very difficult to act according to these principles in the relationship with them. Moffett (1969) suggests that most casework principles are in fact rules of thumb for dealing with people, and I would add that they are largely defensive rules of thumb. They help the worker to defend himself against the often negative (though occasionally strongly positive) feelings which such clients arouse within him. And when writers like Hollis suggest that the aim in working with such clients ought to be to help them strengthen their defences against their impulses, it often seems that the procedures she advocates are rather attempts by the worker to strengthen his defences against the invasion of these strong emotions so threatening to his professional ego.

Leighton (1969) makes an interesting contrast between what is recognized as moral behaviour by writers of the Existential school, and the attitudes expressed in casework techniques. Suggesting that there is an increasing acceptance of such moral values as allowing people personal autonomy, treating them as human beings, searching for creative development and openness in relationships, he contrasts this with the authoritarian objective, diagnostic and manipulative aspects of casework treatment. He poses the question why professional techniques should be at odds with moral values. My suggestion is that this has been so because many people who come to social workers are themselves closed, defensive and manipulative, so that they can influence us towards behaving in a way that expresses their disowned feelings. With such people it is not sufficient for the worker to be open, undemanding and undefended, because the needs of these clients are distorted and restrictive, involving the worker in their defences against themselves. Professional techniques and principles are ways of combating the pressure such people put on us to behave in ways that would be in contradiction to our values. But can we be satisfied with such a defensive system? Is it not possible to find a positive way, in each relationship, of expressing our valuation of our clients through the way we behave towards them? Leighton is right to suggest that we will not find ways of doing this in the writings of Existential moralists, but nor will we do so by hiding behind a wall of professional techniques based on objectivity and non-involvement.

In the first chapter I suggested that clients were able to involve the worker in a role which expressed their disowned feelings by means of defensive manoeuvres. When we consider the helping role of the worker in relation to such clients, we have to answer questions about the way in which the worker can meet these manoeuvres. To what extent is it helpful to challenge a defensive manoeuvre? To what extent is it safe to do so? Certainly some clients are able to make the worker feel that it would be neither helpful nor safe to act otherwise than in the role they have selected for him. Here is an example of such a person.

MRS GEORGE

Mrs George was forty-two years old. She had married young, and her marriage had been unsuccessful. Her husband had turned increasingly to drink, and she told me that she had sought the help of a social worker who had eventually advised her to separate from him. This she had done, but not long afterwards the middle one of her three sons, Ian, then aged thirteen, had started to give her trouble. He refused to go to school, stayed in bed, and quarrelled and fought with her. He was twice removed from home after incidents between him and his mother, and eventually he was sent to a residential school. Although he did quite well at the school, the same pattern of behaviour started up not long after he returned home. By then I was the social worker concerned with the family,

49

and I took the action of recommending that he should return to the school on the basis of Mrs George's complaints about him. Quite soon, Mrs George was willing to have him home again, but within a few weeks the same thing happened, and I found him lodgings. After a while he returned home at his mother's request.

By this time it was fairly clear to me what was happening between Ian and his mother. His lazy and dirty behaviour, which was very like his father's earlier conduct, seemed to reflect a part of Mrs George's personality that she strenuously disowned. She had transmitted this part of herself first into her husband, and then, almost as soon as she left him, into Ian. Although she fought vigorously with them over their behaviour, she was all the time intensifying it, and she depended on them to carry this part of her and express it for her. Removing Ian from home achieved very little for him or for her. She soon needed him back, and he still needed to go back. Since it served no constructive purpose, it should have been easy for me to decide to oppose Mrs George's attempts to have Ian removed in future, but it was not.

The reason for this was that Mrs George always presented her request for Ian to be removed as the most acute crisis. She never seemed to come unless Ian's behaviour was so completely out of control that something had to be done at once. The crisis had always reached unmanageable proportions, and Ian's acting out had passed the bounds of what was tolerable. A period of lazy or dirty behaviour would end in an outbreak of violence, and she would tell me about this in such a way as to make it clear that she had waited till the last possible moment to come in, and that she could not stand any more from him. She presented the crisis in such a way that it seemed as if one of them would kill the other if they were left together, so some immediate action was called for to separate them.

I had a strong feeling that Mrs George provoked these crises with Ian. She seemed to let him become lazy and dirty and then challenge him in such an angry way that he was provoked into a fight with her. However I had a great resistance to suggesting to Mrs George that this was what happened. I felt that there must be a very depressed, lazy and dirty side of her personality of which she was very afraid, and that she would not be able to tolerate being confronted with it. Her anger, her anxiety and her threat of being on the point of breakdown over Ian made me feel that it would be very dangerous to draw attention to this side of her personality. She always seemed to be under too much stress to bear these feelings in herself. In any case, the situation between herself and Ian always appeared to be too urgent to contemplate the discussion of such feelings.

One day after Ian had returned home from the lodgings Mrs George came to see me looking really ill and exhausted. She said that she was sick with worry over Ian, and would have come in to see me before if she had not found it so humiliating to do so. He had given up his job, and had been lying in bed all day, refusing to work, getting very dirty, and making the house filthy. On top of this, there had been a terrible row the previous evening between him and one of his brothers. Mrs George had come between them, and Ian had hit her. He had then picked up a poker and thrown it at his brother, and it had stuck in his chest. She said that this was more than she could stand, and although she had tried not to bother me about Ian's behaviour, she just could not go on after this.

Her account of the fight between Ian and his brother

appalled me, and my first reaction was to feel that if Ian went so far as to impale a member of his family with a poker he could not possibly be allowed to continue to live within the household. However, I managed to take up with Mrs George her reluctance to come in before this incident, suggesting that she really wanted to cope with Ian if she possibly could. I reminded her that every time Ian had gone away from home she had wanted him back, and said I thought she still really wanted him with her. Although Mrs George still continued to talk of Ian's difficult behaviour, her complaints became less violent, and it was even possible to suggest that she really wanted to deal with these difficulties herself, rather than to have Ian taken away again. Quite suddenly, she said she felt a terrible failure with Ian, but after all other people had failed with him as well. I suggested that I in particular had failed, as any actions in arranging for him to return to school and finding him lodgings had not had any effect on his behaviour. I said I thought all these comings and goings had only made Mrs George feel more of a failure. At about this point her whole appearance began to change, and she complained less about him. She compared Ian with her husband, saying how like him he was becoming. I suggested that I had acted like the social worker who had dealt with her difficulties with her husband. Mrs George confirmed that she had been advised to separate from her husband, but said she had never regretted this. However, she then began to talk about Ian's good qualities, and said that there had been an improvement in him since he had come home. When she finally left the office, she said that she wanted to continue as long as possible, as Ian's brother would soon be going into the Army, and then she thought his behaviour would improve.

Once again, Mrs George had managed to make his crisis sound so frightening that some instant solution in terms of my intervention was necessary. She made it seem that for me to fail to take action would be to condone an act of attempted fratricide. If I did nothing, I might have someone's death on my conscience before another night went by. On the other hand, several of the things she said contained hints of her feelings of being a failure as a mother and very much wishing that she could deal with these situations in her family herself. By drawing attention to her mixed feelings about what she was asking me to do, I seemed almost to my own surprise to create the possibility in her mind of continuing to keep Ian within the family.

Mrs George's problem with Ian really reflected her own difficulty in reconciling two parts of her personality, the one she presented to me in interviews and the one that was represented by Ian and his behaviour. She dealt with her bad, dirty and lazy side by disowning it and transmitting it into Ian, but even this was not safe enough for her. She and Ian were bound together by their mutual dependence and their guilt about the things they did to each other. Mrs George tried to detach herself altogether from Ian and what he represented and he used me to bring about this split. Her defensive manoeuvre consisted in creating a frightening situation within her family and then threatening me with the danger of total war between the two parties who represented the two sides of herself. In a situation where such a war had really broken out, and blows were being struck, it seemed unreasonable or even dangerous to try to get Mrs George to look at the problem in terms of the feelings that she was disowning. However, it was possible to get her to look at what she was getting me to do, and the fact that it did not reflect all her feelings about Ian. On this occasion the crisis passed, and Ian's behaviour improved for a time, and after this it was possible to help Mrs George through similar crises. With each one I was able to put to her a little more about her contribution to Ian's behaviour, and although there were many subsequent ups and downs in their relationship, and comings and goings by Ian after his period under supervision ended, he and his mother have now had three years in which they have not turned to a social worker with a crisis in their relationship.

This I would regard as progress because the way that Mrs George was able to use her relationship with social workers was so destructive to herself and her family. It was designed to protect her from the dangers of a family war, but when these dangers were faced they were found to be more bearable than she had feared. My actions in splitting her off from Ian merely confirmed her phantasies about the danger that they would destroy each other, and her guilt about her failure as a mother to him. Once this splitting role was challenged she found that she could tolerate and deal with the difficult parts of herself both in her and in Ian better than she had imagined.

The difficulty of working with Mrs George might well be analysed in terms of her impulsiveness, her poor ego functioning or her immaturity, but I think that this would really miss the point. The difficulty about her was what she got me to do. It was not so much that it was hard to get her to get insight into her behaviour as that it was hard to avoid acting out her defences against the parts of herself that she feared. Her problem was really expressed in her relationship with me, in the way she used me to split off the part of herself that was represented by Ian. Any

understanding I had of her behaviour and any plans I made
to try and help her were undermined by the invasion of her
fears about the dangers of a conflict between herself and
her son.

I would describe someone like Mrs George as a disruptive
person because of her ability to influence a social worker
to behave in a way which reflected her feelings and phantasies more than it reflected his judgment of the needs of
the case. The ability to do this is important, because casework theorists have tended to assume that it is possible
objectively to define certain types of people who can
benefit from certain kinds of help. For instance, Hollis
(1964) suggests that whether or not a client will benefit
from insight-giving techniques depends on his level of
anxiety and ability to form mature relationships. I would
suggest that the question of how much a client can be
helped in a particular way must considerably depend on
how much the worker is able to deal with the feelings
that he is forced to bear in his relationship with the client.
In the case of Mrs George it was my own fear of the
conflicts within herself and her family that I had to
overcome before I could behave in a way that was helpful
to her. If the worker can withstand the force of the feeling
that the client puts into him and is prepared to share with
the client all the difficulty and pain of working through
this feeling, and showing that it can be borne, then perhaps it is safe to try anything in helping any client, so
long as the worker knows himself and the client well
enough to feel that they can both together face the feelings
involved.

There is a tradition in casework theory that people who
are judged to be deficient in ego strength and impulse-
control and who tend to act out their feelings should be

'sustained' and 'supported' rather than encouraged to look at the irrational parts of their personalities. This policy fails to take account of the fact that disruptive people often put a social worker in a position where he has to choose between behaving in a way which, though superficially 'supportive', actually confirms all the worst elements in a destructive pattern of behaviour, or doing something which challenges this pattern. The problem is to find a way of doing the challenging thing, while at the same time providing support in the form of helping the client to bear the fear and pain of facing something in himself that he has been trying hard to avoid.

My suggestion is that finding a way to do this is not best thought of in terms of matching a set of 'treatment techniques' to a set of 'psychosocial symptoms'. It is more a question of understanding how the role the client is trying to get the worker to play reflects a defensive or distorted way of relating to people, and finding a way of relating towards him that helps him to discover that this way of relating is not as necessary for his self-preservation as he feels it to be.

The difficulties of doing this with disruptive people are enormous. Here is an example of an attempt to work with a couple of such people over a period of time.

MR AND MRS BARTON

Mr and Mrs Barton have now been married for five years. I knew them both briefly before their marriage, and I went to their wedding. For three years after that I suppose I saw them on average about twice a week.

When I first met him, Mr Barton had just come out of Borstal. He had previously been in Approved School, and the interval between these two long periods of residential training had been only six months. He had five court appearances for housebreaking and larceny, as well as others for lesser offences.

He was the second in a family of five, and his father had left his mother many years previously. She was a dried-up, worn-out, negative sort of woman, who always gave the impression of being cheerless, miserable and complaining. She was always in debt, and was particularly prone to breaking into her pre-payment meters, though she had never been prosecuted for this. I was told that Mr Barton had often given her the proceeds of his offences to help her out. His elder sister had married and moved away; there were two young sisters and a brother, who was still at school, living in the home, which was a drab place. Mr Barton was twenty years old.

In my first four interviews with Mr Barton he seemed very anxious to please and to give a good impression, much in the manner in which he had been trained to behave in Borstal. Within three months of coming home he told me that he had met a girl to whom he had taken a great liking, and that she had an illegitimate child. Within a month they had decided to get married, but his mother opposed the idea. She quickly changed her mind, and I was introduced to the girl. The wedding was originally planned for several months ahead, but it was soon put forward. A few weeks before the wedding, Mr Barton became very concerned about one of his fiancée's relationships with a young man she had known before she met him, and he persuaded me to go and see them both about this, though she eventually reassured him that she was no longer interested in this man. He came in three days before the wedding to borrow some money for the ring (he said he had missed work for a couple of days with an injury). Finally when I went to his house the following day, I had to witness the consent form which his mother only then signed and even deliver it to the Registrar's office the following morning. After they were married, they went to live with her parents temporarily. Five days later Mr Barton was arrested for housebreaking and remanded in custody.

By the time I saw Mrs Barton, she had already been thrown out of the house by her parents and taken back again the same day. She told me she was expecting a baby, but her mother did not know this.

Immediately after this, I was contacted by a social worker who had known Mrs Barton for some time before her marriage. I was told that Mrs Barton had always been the difficult member of her family. Her parents were hard-working people, but there had always been a stormy relationship between them and Mrs Barton, who was the second in a family of four. She had been assessed as educationally subnormal at school, though her learning had probably been affected by emotional factors, and she had been referred to the Child Guidance Clinic. There was a history of quarrels in the home throughout her adolescence but her mother had readily agreed to her keeping her illegitimate daughter Mary, who was now a year old. The social worker felt it would be advisable for Mrs Barton to leave home as soon as possible because of the longstanding difficulties there.

While Mr Barton was still on remand, his wife quarrelled with her parents and went to live with his family. Within a week she had to return home because her daughter was not settling down. I provided the transport. When Mr Barton finally came up in Court again, he was recalled to

Borstal. He was very angry with me because I did nothing to try to prevent this. This was the first time I had seen him express any anger.

Within a month of this, Mrs Barton rang me up to say there had been a major row at her house, and she would have to leave. When I arrived there I found her apparently fairly calm, packing her belongings. Her mother saw me separately. She was a very strange colour and trembling with rage. She said she felt that if her daughter stayed in the house for a moment longer, she would run her through with a knife. She had already hit her. I was convinced that something had to be done, and duly arranged for Mrs Barton to go to a hostel with Mary. When I called back to fetch her, there was quite a difference in the atmosphere, and both Mrs Barton and her mother were crying when we left. It was a long and exhausting journey to the hostel, with all her belongings and the baby, and by the time I had unpacked for her and driven back to my office it was late in the afternoon. The same evening, Mrs Barton left the hostel and went home, where her mother welcomed her back. I had to go to fetch her belongings from the hostel some days later.

By this time, the pattern of events should have been becoming clear to me. I knew something of Mr Barton's relationship with his mother, and the sort of person it had made him. Within a few days of his marriage he had been stealing to provide for his wife as he had previously done for his mother. While he was away, his wife had been turned out of the house three times by her parents, and I had already had several long journeys with all her possessions in my car. (I should explain that this was a van, something which made physically possible a number of the extraordinary things the Bartons got me to do.) I should have been able to see that I was being given a role towards them which was in some way related to their previous experiences with their parents, and which was to have an important function in their relationship with each other.

I am not normally addicted to transporting furniture, but after knowing the Bartons for a short time I seemed to take it for granted that I did this for them. Nor do I often spend very long looking for accommodation for my clients, but before Mr Barton returned home from Borstal, I had spent a good deal of time doing this, and had got them a flat. Not only did I move their furniture in for them, I also obtained other bits and pieces for the flat, and went on shifting things about for some time after they had got established there. My records of my early visits to them after he came home are full of concern about their welfare and hopeful comments on their progress. The baby was born soon afterwards, a boy, of whom I was almost as proud as they were.

Why should I have played this thoroughly paternal role towards them? What persuaded me to rush about several times a week for many weeks with my car full of mattresses and stoves and even baths? It seems that this was because they were two young people who had had thoroughly damaging and destructive relationships with their parents, who therefore made me feel that I had a parental role to play towards them, in which I could by my attitudes and actions do something to repair the damage that had been done to them during their childhoods. They made me feel that what I was doing was helpful, essential even. They conveyed to me their desperate hopes of a new and different life together, under my benevolent supervision. But at the same time as they were giving me the role of a good parent, their dependence, their ambivalence and the other bad features of their earlier relationships ensured that I had to play this role on their terms.

Both Mr and Mrs Barton had been difficult people before their marriage, and their life together had got off to the worst possible start. It must have confirmed their grimmest fears about themselves and each other when Mr Barton went back to Borstal within a week of their wedding. The weeks after he returned were ones of the utmost anxiety for them, yet during which they were hoping against hope for some miracle by which their lives were to be transformed, and they were to become different people. This anxiety and this hope communicated itself strongly to me, and I played right into their most unrealistic phantasies. Rushing around like some demented fairy godfather, showering them with second-hand furniture, my actions reflected the most distorted elements in their expectation of married life; that its success depended largely on the provision of a suitable environment, that their previous difficulties might just disappear if they were not mentioned, that one way of helping this was to rush about at the highest possible speed. These phantasies were to dog my future work with the Bartons, and the fact that I started my relationship with them by acting them out on their behalf was a very hard thing for me to live down. Once the Bartons had got themselves a fairy godfather they didn't easily give him up.

Something had to go wrong before long, as we all really knew. Mrs Barton began to complain bitterly of loneliness, saying that while her husband was at work she was a prisoner in the flat, which she didn't like anyway, and to press for a move somewhere else. Next there was a 'phone call from Mr Barton to say that he had left the very good job he had had for two months. He asked to see me at my office. After an elaborate and unconvincing account of how he had come to leave, he suggested that he would be most likely to settle in a job such as he might get in a hotel or on a boat. I managed not to go along with this phantasy, but instead suggested that certain factors in his home situation had not made things easy for him. For instance, Mrs Barton had been complaining about her life and the flat a great deal. He denied that this had influenced him, but went on after a bit to acknowledge that he had been concerned at the way she got through his money. She spent everything he gave her (which was virtually all he earned) and then came to him during the week for money for the gas and electricity meters. I said this must be all the more disturbing for him because it was very like the sort of experience he had had with his mother. Mr Barton gave me a blank look for a moment (in which I think he was suppressing his anger at my comment) and then said this was perfectly true and exactly what had happened with his mother. In fact, in those days he had been earning about £20 a week and his mother had got through the lot. We then talked about his wife's reaction to his losing his job, and he told me that she had not been at all upset, and even almost pleased about it. He would have preferred her to be angry. We discussed the fact that she liked having him at home, and did not mind being on assistance, and he gloomily agreed that this too was like his mother. Before he left I acknowledged his having told both his wife and myself about losing his job; he had never done this before, always keeping it secret and committing offences to cover up his loss of earnings. At least he had broken this pattern.

This interview is a good example of Mr Barton's ambivalence towards me, and the influence it had on my behaviour. He started by testing me out with what was probably a fictitious account of his loss of his job, and an unrealistic solution to the problem. I managed to resist falling into this trap, and instead succeeded in getting him to relate this failure to his past pattern of behaviour, his expectations of his relationship with his wife, and their partial disappointment. No doubt in screwing up the courage to tell me about losing the job Mr Barton had had very mixed feelings; partly hoping that I would go on playing fairy godfather and get him a lovely hotel job, partly hoping that I would be realistic and help him face some of his feelings about the fact that his new life was not everything that he had dreamed of. On the one hand I was able to fill the latter role, and thus start to break the pattern I had been establishing. And yet, soon after this interview I began to slip back into my previous role. Although I refused to adopt a protective attitude over his having to go to draw assistance (something which he strongly resisted doing) I saw him three times during the next week, without ever really following up with him or his wife the matters which had been raised. When he started work again, my visits once more became benevolent affairs in which difficulties in their relationship were touched upon rather than squarely faced. Within two weeks he presented me with a doubtful story about being underpaid one week, and I feebly lent him some money to make up his wages. This was repaid immediately, but a week later he had lost his job.

This time Mr Barton made no excuses. He was depressed and said he could not understand himself. He knew it had been his own fault; he thought he needed to see a psychiatrist. I acknowledged that he was facing the fact that these difficulties were of his own making, and that he had never done this before when he had lost jobs. He said that there was now something new which he had not been doing before he was married. Previously he had always got another job straight away, or got into trouble; now he seemed to want to stay at home all the time. I pointed out that he seemed to be suggesting that there was something wrong deep down inside him, but perhaps there was also something wrong between him and his wife. He said he didn't want to blame her, but I pressed him to talk more about their relationship. Eventually he said that they quarrelled a lot over the children. Recently they had had a row because he felt she was neglecting the baby, John, not feeding him, or leaving him wet. We talked about his very strong feelings about John, how he identified with him, and felt very angry if his wife seemed to be neglecting him. He also mentioned rows about the daughter, Mary, whom his wife seemed to be protecting from him. He resented not being allowed to behave as a father to Mary, and I said I realized that this was partly because he was not Mary's father. He said all this did not seem to tie in with his losing his job, and I suggested that perhaps he wanted to be at home to keep an eye on his wife, and to see that John got a fair deal from her. He wanted to be with her all the time, but his being there led to arguments. When we had discussed this I arranged to see them both to take it up again.

When this interview took place they began to admit that they were fighting against each other, with Mr Barton and John against Mrs Barton and Mary. She told me that she had threatened to leave with Mary the previous week, and that this had infuriated him because she was prepared to leave John behind. After this interview, Mr Barton rang me very angrily to accuse me of telling his mother-in-law everything that had been happening between them. When I denied this, he accused his wife of the same thing, and they had a considerable row about it. Within a week, they told me that they had made contact with his father, whom he had not seen for several years, and had decided to move to the town where he was living, about a hundred miles away.

It should have been very clear to me that they were running away from the difficulties they had just began to discuss with me, and I should have confronted them with this. Instead I started by failing to challenge the idea at all effectively, and ended by colluding with it. On the eve of their departure I was rushing about making all the financial arrangements for them to leave. The fairy godfather was back in business, playing along with their phantasies, and failing to notice that one of these was that I didn't want to know them any more. I was succeeding in compounding rejection with collusion, and confirming for the Bartons that when they came face to face with their real feelings, they couldn't tolerate them, and nor could I.

Within a fortnight they were back. Everything had gone wrong because Mrs Barton had been homesick, and had made herself ill. Now they were living at Mr Barton's mother's house, temporarily. A week later they were thrown out of there, and I went to plead with Mrs Barton's parents to have them. They eventually agreed to have them for a week. I picked up their belongings, what was left of them, and stored them at my office. The next week was spent rushing round looking for a flat, with her parents nagging to get them out. We found one, but within a few days they had to leave. Eventually he found another, within a few minutes walk of my office. We moved their things in there together, and I spent the next couple of weeks getting them furniture.

By now I was beginning to be aware of what was happening between me and them, but I was still very helpless in face of it. When they finally got into their flat, I made them talk about what all these crises had been about. I said I knew that it was no coincidence that they had found themselves homeless after trying unsuccessfully to live first with each of Mr Barton's parents and then with Mrs Barton's. I said I thought that they were both still very involved with their parents, and I realized it was a very painful experience to be thrown out by each of them in turn. What I did not say was anything about the way they had used me, or how I had allowed myself to behave. In the face of their fears about themselves, I still felt compelled to hover over them as guardian of their marriage, to whom they could turn whenever anything went wrong. And they did.

They had hardly begun to settle in the new flat when they moved to another in the same house. There began a series of fights between them which increased in intensity as the weeks went by. They kept leaving each other; she would go back to her mother with Mary, or he would go to his mother's house. These separations never lasted more than a few hours, but they would always be referred to me, so that I had to interview both sides and effect a reconciliation. Meanwhile, he was not working, and they were desperately short of money. She spent what they had recklessly. She became scruffy, and so did the children. Then he broke into the meters in the house and they were again threatened with eviction and homelessness. This time I found myself even more involved, with the landlady, with the council who were half promising to house them, with their parents who were half encouraging them to separate. When they were eventually given notice to quit, and the council did not house them, it seemed both to them and to me as if it was I who had failed them. He found another flat, even closer to my office. The quarrels between them increased, in frequency and intensity.

By now it was two years since I had first met Mr Barton. How had I got myself into this role with him and his wife? Right from the start, they seemed to appoint me to preside over their marriage as custodian of the phantasy that it was going to be the answer to everything, the end of all the unhappiness they had both experienced and the upset they had caused to others. I had allowed myself to act in a way which showed I accepted this role, and in my own phantasy I was even willing to do so. The justification had been, and now continued to be, the attitudes of the Bartons' parents. Mr Barton's mother now encouraged him to leave his wife and return to live with her, bringing his son with him. Mrs Barton's mother was prepared to accept her and Mary back if they separated. Both parents rejected and blamed everything on to the other partner. Both seemed to collude with the part of the Bartons which now wanted to forget everything that had been wrong with their relationships before their marriage, and to make everything that had gone wrong seem to be because of the failure of the marriage.

This seemed to be typical of what had gone wrong for both of the Bartons all through their childhood and up to their marriage. Mr Barton's mother could accept him as the son who worked hard and gave her all his money; she hadn't wanted to know about the bad side of him, the housebreaker, the Borstal boy. Mrs Barton's mother had accepted her as the mother of an illegitimate baby, but she had quarrelled endlessly with her and rejected her as an angry, complaining adolescent. Both of them were now putting their bad side into the marriage, and withholding their acceptable side from each other altogether. Mr Barton was work-shy, bad tempered, sometimes violent. Mrs Barton was scruffy, miserable, a bad manager. As their bad selves, they were telling me and each other that they could not possibly be tolerated, they could not continue to stay married, they would rather go back to the safety of their old relationships with their parents.

What I was trying to do during this period was to show them what they were doing to each other. In fact, in the very many long interviews I had with them, it often seemed that I was succeeding in doing this. What I entirely failed to do was to recognize or confront them with what they were doing to me. In their anger about the failure of their marriage to turn them into different people, they had turned against the person who seemed to have promised them that it would. Since I had accepted the role of fairy godfather, and the dream had not come true, they were making me take the consequences, and I was still allowing them to do this. They were still using their parents as an escape from the bad side of themselves in their marriage, but equally they were using me as a protection against the other realities of their relationship. Because they could come to me for reconciliation every time they quarrelled, they never had to face their dependence on each other; they never had to think twice about having a row and splitting up. Just as I had originally helped support their phantasy that their marriage was the answer to their problems, now I was helping support the phantasy that their marriage was a complete failure, and they were a burden to each other. Whatever I might say in interviews was belied by my actions in repeatedly rushing out to bring them together. And instead of moderating their acting out, this seemed to intensify it. The very things that I feared, and the fear which drove me to take such a protective role, began to happen. They got hopelessly into arrears with the rent. Mr Barton took an overdose of tablets, and nearly died. They both took money from their meter, and Mr Barton was arrested.

The Bartons had been involved in a defensive manoeuvre in which my actions were intended to protect them from themselves. Having had such high hopes of their marriage, it was not easy for them to acknowledge that there was now no magical way left of escaping from the problems which lay within their personalities. Neither of them really believed that the answer lay in going back to their parents, but it was an easier answer than facing the bad things in themselves and each other. They got me to act out for them the part of themselves that did not want to let go of their marriage, but in such a way that I made it plain that I did not really feel they could make it work on their own. By being so protective, by showing that I felt they needed me so much, I seemed to confirm that they were as bad as they felt themselves to be. Therefore this form of manoeuvre was ineffective as a defence and my behaviour confirmed their worst fears about themselves.

Mr Barton was in custody for a time, although eventually the Court allowed him his liberty. This time served to confront Mrs Barton with some of her dependence on her husband and gave me a chance to reassess my position. I was aware that I had allowed myself to be involved too much in their lives, but I felt that it was sufficient for me to announce my intention not to get mixed up in their financial muddles in future. In fact, I recorded in a treatment plan that 'I still feel that my role is to cope with the emotional turmoil by helping them to recognize their own part in each other's behaviour and showing that I feel their marriage can continue in spite of the weight of emotional problems which it contains.' I was still too full of the Bartons' fears about themselves to let go.

After this they stopped running away from each other, but the other difficulties persisted. They had their electricity supply cut off, and they were evicted for arrears of rent. However, this time they were accommodated by the council in a flat which, though unsatisfactory in many ways, was a much better type of accommodation than they had ever had before. Mr Barton got a good job and kept it, Mrs Barton began to keep the flat a bit cleaner. I started to visit less frequently, and there were much fewer emergency visits to the office. When I saw them, I was able to be less protective towards them.

Very slowly, things began to change. They were beginning to face the real problems of two difficult people living together, and they were beginning to let me allow them to do so. One day when I went to their flat, Mrs Barton started to talk about difficulties she was having with John, while Mr Barton sat looking very gloomy. She said John was obstinate, and seemed to enjoy soiling himself and messing up the flat. He had got worse since they had moved there. I suggested that this perhaps reflected her anxieties about keeping the place clean, and her fear that she might get it into a mess as she had her other flats. She was able to accept this up to a point, and even tell me that she herself had been messy in the same way as a child. Mr Barton joined in the conversation at this point, and then suddenly became very angry with his wife. He said he was working very hard at his job, and how miserable it was to have to come home to her. She was miserable and useless, and his life at present would be quite happy if it wasn't for her. She said he always came home in a bad temper and would not speak to him. I suggested that it must be hard for them to discover that even when they had no material or financial problems, they were still miserable or angry people. To my surprise, Mr Barton acknowledged that he was a thoroughly bad-tempered person, but added that his wife deliberately provoked him, so that although he managed to be pleasant to other people, he was always nasty to her. We talked about this and she said that they were as bad as ever with each other, and furthermore they were 'having nothing to do with each other'. When I asked about this Mr Barton said they hardly ever made love, and he thought that there was something wrong with her, because she seemed to have no feelings. She confirmed that at present she could not enjoy making love, and he said scornfully that she should see a doctor, and it was her fault that she had not had this put right. She began to cry, and said she wanted to make love sometimes, but he refused. He denied this hotly, but she insisted that it was true. I suggested that Mr Barton felt very bad about the fact that his wife did not seem to enjoy making love with him, and he acknowledged this, saying it made him feel hopeless and useless. When she was disbelieving about this, he reminded her of an incident when he had cried, but she refused to remember this. He said he found it easier to discuss such matters than she did, and this was why he did not show his feelings so much as she did in talking about it. I suggested that it was easier for him to discuss it because he saw it as her problem, but I did not accept this and saw it as his problem also. I suggested that his fears about her lack of feelings contributed to the fact that they made love so seldom. He accepted this up to a point, but Mrs Barton remained tearful and angry, saying that she had not realized how he felt about her. She said that she felt a failure as a wife, and as we talked about this it was clear that he felt exactly the same about his part as a husband.

Soon after this the Bartons were rehoused, and it was not until some months later, after the dust had settled from this fresh upheaval, that we returned to this subject. Mrs Barton suddenly announced her intention of going to the Family Planning Clinic, something she had steadfastly refused to do before. When I asked them about this, she said that her husband opposed her going, but he refused to discuss the matter at all. He had nothing to say, even when she told me that he would not make love with her at all at that time. She had thought that it had been her fault that they did not make love, but now she thought it was his.

After this she brought considerable pressure to bear on the Health Visitor and her doctor over the question of family planning, insisting that she was very much afraid of becoming pregnant again, but her husband was opposing her going to the Clinic. She asked them to tackle her husband about this. The question was referred back to me (within a fortnight of the previous interview) and I raised it again with them. I pointed out that Mr Barton seemed to be dodging the subject which he had previously told me he was well able to discuss, and that Mrs Barton was raising the question of family planning when they were not making love, whereas she had avoided it when they were. Mrs Barton said that things were much better between them, and to my surprise, her husband agreed to her going to the Clinic. However, when she finally did go, she soon abandoned the contraceptive method which was recommended. When I suggested that she had only raised the question to draw attention to their sexual difficulties, she cheerfully accepted this, but assured me that these were now a thing of the past.

This piece of manipulation by Mrs Barton was thoroughly typical. An emotional problem in their relationship was brought up in a disguised form, and presented in such a way as to demand a solution from myself or the Family Planning Clinic. On this occasion, however, they found their own solution, perhaps because they did not succeed in getting me to rush in and impose mine upon them. Furthermore, the problem itself and their recognition of it seemed to have reflected some increase in their maturity and their ability to face the real issues in their relationship. They were no longer so entirely preoccupied with their primitive emotions and the question of whether life together was possible.

I found that I was seeing them fortnightly, and I began not to expect crises in the intervals between visits. I no longer felt the need to protect them from each other or the outside world, and I made up my mind not to do so again. However, I realized that it would be difficult if one of the old situations arose again to keep to this resolve. Once one has been a fairy godfather it's a hard thing to get to be an ordinary social worker again.

One day when I visited them, the interview started quite cheerfully, but after a while Mrs Barton began to grouse and I asked if anything was up. They then told me that at the weekend there had been a big row because she had come back from town with John in a bad way,

73

having lost one of his teeth in a fall, and Mr Barton blamed her for this and threw her out of the house. She had been to the police station, and the police had been up and talked to them both. Mr Barton had produced a lot of neighbours who said that she was cruel to the children, and Mrs Barton in turn had convinced the police that there were no marks or bruises on them and that they were healthy and well cared-for. In the end the police seemed to have given both sides a good talking-to. Mr Barton was now complaining that his wife did not get enough help with the children from any of the authorities, particularly from the Health Visitor, that they should be at a nursery school, that she should have a home help, that they should get better medical treatment and so on. However, as this was discussed, the fact emerged that the row involving the police had occurred two weekends previously, and that ever since then Mrs Barton's care of the children had improved considerably, and Mr Barton had taken more trouble with them too. I noticed that the house was looking very smart, and Mr Barton added that the children were sleeping better, and behaving better. I drew attention to these improvements, and to his complaints that they were not getting enough help from the authorities. I suggested that he was saying that nowadays they were expected to do all these things for themselves, without all the kinds of help they had had in the past. I pointed out that before I would almost certainly have been involved in the row between them, but that many of the things they had done recently proved that they no longer needed this. Perhaps there was some regret on both sides that this kind of relationship had ended, but I thought on the whole they felt it was a good thing that they were so much better able to solve their own problems, as they had found in the past fortnight. Mr and Mrs Barton seemed gradually to accept this, and told me about other improvements in the children. As I was going they gave me some vegetables from their garden, agreeing cheerfully that this was a more satisfactory thing to be doing than asking me for money as they used to do so frequently in the past. This was several months ago, and they have not involved me in crises since then.

Before they were married Mr and Mrs Barton gave a lot of trouble to a lot of people. Since their marriage they seem to have troubled few people except me. At times they have been more or less a full-time job on their own. One year Mrs Barton came to my house on Boxing Day to tell me she was leaving her husband. He used to be able to find me to tell me about the latest crisis even when I was digging on my allotment. When they were homeless, they stored their furniture in my office and virtually lived in my car. Everything that happened to them, happened to me.

This pattern was established right at the start of their marriage, when they convinced me that they were two thoroughly disturbed people desperately seeking a satisfactory relationship for the first time in their lives. They involved me with a parental function and a responsibility for their marriage, such that I felt that in order to be a good parent, I had to put an endless amount of energy and concern into supervising their relationship with each other. When things went wrong, I had to be at hand to sort them out, whether they had lost a wage packet, failed to pay the rent or nearly killed each other. They used me to protect them from their primitive, infantile emotions which they feared would destroy the relationship in which they secretly placed all their trust. For years I have

75

played this game with them, and if I have managed to stop playing it now, it is because they have allowed me to do so.

The parental role which I took, although it was consciously aimed at being the exact opposite of the relationship they had had with their own parents, has reproduced many of the worst features of these relationships. I have been inconsistent and overprotective. I have often said one thing and done another. I have colluded with many of their most distorted phantasies about themselves and each other.

I don't believe that I am by nature a fairy godfather. I think that my behaviour towards them has reflected a very desperate need on their part for a parental figure of some kind, but because of their very damaging early experiences, their phantasy about what such a figure should be was such that they were able to influence me to fill this extraordinary role. There must, of course, be something in me that wanted to collude with their expectations, and prevented me from challenging them years ago. For several years my working life was often completely disrupted by them, and I deserved to have it disrupted. But there were some positive elements in my role. For all their eccentricities, fairy godfathers really do care, and I think the Bartons could tell this.

At one time, Mr Barton had not survived more than six months out of an institution since leaving approved school. It is now two years since he was last in court, and four years since his last period of institutional training. Mrs Barton is a reasonably competent mother who no longer causes concern to medical authorities. Mr Barton, who at one time had never held a job for more than a few weeks, has not been out of work for a year. In many ways the

Bartons have succeeded in realizing the best hopes that they could reasonably have had for themselves. Their disruptive influence on me, while it always seemed to be based on the hope of something better than the life they were having, was mainly motivated by the fear of something very much worse. Looking back on my work with them, much of it has been comic in its collusion with their phantasies. However, I have managed to be fairly consistent in treating them as worthwhile people, whose problems were real, and whose marriage was worth preserving. Perhaps with such contradictory difficult and disruptive people as the Bartons there is no way of working which does not involve some degree of collusion. I could not challenge one phantasy without seeming to confirm another. In trying to avoid one role which they were forcing upon me, I fell into another equally distorted one.

Mr and Mrs Barton were disruptive people for the same sort of reasons as Mr Peterson and Mrs George. Their influence on my actions as a social worker was directed at defending them from the things they most feared in themselves. However, while I played the role they gave me, I did not succeed in preventing the recurrent crises which were the feature of their lives. It was only when they were able to face life without the protection that they seemed to demand from me, then they began to realize their true potential as a married couple. There was a helpful role for me to play, but I could not find how to play it adequately while I was acting out their defences against the bad things in their marriage. Once they could face being their true selves, they were no longer such disruptive people.

Suggestions for further reading

For a full version of what I have called the accepted theory of the client-worker relationship, see Hollis (1964) and Ferard and Hunnybun (1962). Special aspects of this subject are developed in the Association of Psychiatric Social Workers' symposium 'Relationship in Casework'. Timms (1964) places more emphasis on agency function, and in this respect is more in line with the way of thinking about the relationship that I have put forward. However, there is relatively little written about the casework relationship from the point of view of the interaction between client and worker. Grinker comes nearest to this approach. In his definition, 'transactional . . . implies a relationship of two or more individuals within a specific environment which includes both of them, not as distinct or separate individuals, but only as they are in relatedness with each other within a specific system'. However, it does not imply, in his use of the word, that a process of unconscious emotional communication takes place between client and worker by which the former is able to influence the behaviour of the latter, and this is an essential part of the

79

way of thinking that I have suggested. For a much fuller development of the notions of family interaction which I introduce in the first chapter, N. W. Ackerman's two books (1958 and 1966) are valuable.

For those who do not want to tackle the works of Freud and Melanie Klein, Guntrip (1961) provides a very good introduction to theories. As the title suggests, the book looks at interaction from the point of view of a psychological theory based on the notion of personality structure, with the consequences to which I drew attention in the second chapter. See also I. Wittenberg, (forthcoming in this series). The Family Discussion Bureau's approach to marital interaction can be found in Pincus (1960). But the book which most closely examines the kind of phenomena to which I have drawn attention is Racker (1968). This is not an easy book, and assumes a certain amount of familiarity with psychoanalytic language and theory, but the sections on countertransference in particular give valuable examples of the way patients can communicate feelings to their analysts.

On treatment methods, there is much in Hollis, which is usefully analysed by Moffett (1968). For those interested in the ethics of casework I would recommend Leighton (1969). On the subject of disruptive people, much has been written about immaturity and about problem families, but perhaps the most useful book is A. F. Philp (1963).

Bibliography

ACKERMAN, N. W. (1958) *Psychodynamics of Family Life*, Basic Books.

(1966) *Treating the Troubled Family*, Basic Books.

FERARD, M. L. & HUNNYBUN, N. K. (1962) *Caseworker's Use of Relationships*, Tavistock.

GOLDBERG, E. M. (1963) 'Function and Use of Relationship in Psychiatric Social Work'. In *Relationship in Casework*, Association of Psychiatric Social Workers.

GRINKER, R. R. (1961) *Psychiatric Social Work: Transactional Case Book*, Basic Books

GUNTRIP, H. (1961) *Personality Structure and Human Interaction*, Hogarth.

HOLLIS, F. (1964) *Casework: A Psychosocial Therapy*, Random House.

IRVINE, E. E. (1963) 'Transference and Reality in the Casework Relationship'. In *Relationship in Casework*, Association of Psychiatric Social Workers.

JORDAN, W. J. O. (1968) 'The Transmission of Feelings', *Case Conference*, Vol. 15, No. 8, December.

LAING, R. D. & ESTERSON, A. (1964) *Sanity, Madness and the Family*, Vol. 1, *Families of Schizophrenic*, Tavistock.

LEIGHTON, N. (1969) 'Existential Ethics and Casework Techniques', *Case Conference*, Vol. 16, No. 1, May.

BIBLIOGRAPHY

LLOYD DAVIES, A. B. (1963) 'Psychotherapy and Social Casework'. In *Relationship in Casework*, Association of Psychiatric Social Workers.

MOFFETT, J. (1968) *Concepts in Casework Treatment*, Routledge & Kegan Paul.

PHILP, A. F. (1963) *Family Failure*, Faber.

PINCUS, L. (1962) in Family Discussion Bureau's *The Marital Relationship as a Focus for Casework*, Codicote Press Ltd.

PINCUS, L. & BANNISTER, K. (1965) *'Shared Phantasy in Marital Problems'*, Codicote Press Ltd.

RACKER, H. (1968) *Transference and Countertransference*, Hogarth Press and Institute of Psychoanalysis.

RYLE, G. (1949) *The Concept of Mind*, Hutchinson.

TIMMS, N. (1964) *Social Casework*, Routledge & Kegan Paul.

WITTENBERG, I. (Forthcoming) *Psycho-Analytic Insight and Relationships*, Routledge & Kegan Paul.